THE WAY I SEE IT

All rights reserved. The moral rights of the author have been asserted. No part of this book may be reproduced, stored in a retrieval system or transmitted in any form by any means, electronic, mechanical, copying, recording or otherwise without the prior consent of the publisher.

ISBN: 978-0-6457859-6-8 (paperback)
ISBN: 978-0-6457859-2-0 (e-book)

First edition 2025
Published by Bouley Bay Books, Sydney & Jersey
www.bouleybaybooks.com
Typeset in Australia by Image DTO
imagedto@gmail.com
Cover design by Trish Le Moignan
Copyright © Pamela Ward, United Kingdom (2025)

THE WAY I SEE IT

Pam Ward

Bouley Bay BOOKS

For Isobel, George, Lily, Albie and Adeline
The world and its future belongs to them.
Let's make sure it's still a place of wonder.

Contents

Introduction   1

Isolation   2

1. Memories of Svalbard   5
2. Frozen in Time   6
3. I cried into my ironing today   7
4. This different world   8
5. This time last year   9
6. Riverside Walk   10
7. The name I dare not speak   11
8. Our Sterile Room   12
9. Operation Vaccination   13
10. Night Sky   14
11. Seize the Day   15
12. Forest Walk   16

People   17

13. My Buxom Blackpool Grandma   19
14. Skipping Rope Blues   20
15. My Brother's Birthday   22
16. Peter, my big brother   24
17. Mick   25
18. Fab Four   26
19. A cold, wet Thursday in Grantown   27
20. Caryl   28
21. My Grandma's Story   29
22. Pat   30
23. Snowflakes   32
24. CD Necklace   33
25. Thoughts on Age   34
26. Letter to Rachel Carson   36

We, the Watchers — 37

27. Sky Dance — 38
28. Eagle Eyes — 39
29. View from Space — 40
30. Dark Green Fritillary — 41
31. Willow Warbler — 42
32. Night Visitor — 43
33. Fox Family — 44
34. Thoughts on Sheffield — 45
35. The Hoolock Gibbon – a story of our time — 46
36. The Kite — 48
37. Nethy to Grantown Bike Ride — 49
38. The Mountain Ash — 50
39. Nature's Balm — 51
40. A Close Encounter — 52
41. The Meadow — 54
42. The Treasures of the Mind — 55
43. Winners and Losers — 56
44. On Geese Flying — 57

Acknowledgements — 58

About the Author — 59

Introduction

I have enjoyed writing poetry since my early school days, but the poems in this anthology were born from the ashes of the recent Covid 19 pandemic. The world experienced a seismic shock, when many of us faced events and emotions that changed our perspectives on the world. Uncertainty and anxiety reigned.

During the pandemic we had to adjust to a completely new way of living. We were cut off from normal social interaction. Some of us had little or no contact with close family or friends, other than by electronic means. In Scotland, where I now have my home, for a period of time leaving the country was prohibited.

Against this background of isolation and uncertainty about the future, I started to focus on things I had ignored or put to the back of my mind. Like many others, I began to appreciate the present and look more closely at the natural world. It also triggered memories of people from my past, who had been strong influences and helped shape my personal growth – figures such as my Blackpool Grandma and my older brother Peter.

The anthology is in three sections. The first focuses on the emotions and concerns around the new situations in which we found ourselves. The second looks closely at early influences, such as those people mentioned above. These were often inspired by old photographs, as I rifled through albums. The third section centres on the beauty of the natural world, highlighting some disappearing species such as the Hoolock Gibbon and the frailty of this wonderful planet that we call home.

I hope you enjoy reading the poems.

Isolation

In 2012, I excitedly joined a cruise ship heading north for Svalbard and the edge of the ice pack. The voyage was organised by the National Trust For Scotland and provided a range of activities and lectures alongside other forms of entertainment.

The first poem, *Memories of Svalbard* refers to that journey and was the first time I had considered the possibility of a global pandemic and its impact, when one of the experienced lecturers on the ship alerted us, not to its possibility, but to its probability. Eight years later, on 11 March 2020, the World Health Organisation officially declared the presence of the pandemic we know as COVID 19. And our daily lives changed for ever.

The poems in this section were all written during this period of uncertainty and were my attempts to make sense of what was happening and reflect on the altered patterns of behaviour and range of emotions I experienced, especially during lockdown when we were isolated from others. We were not even allowed to travel from Scotland to England, where my close family lived.

In most cases, the process of composing the poems had a therapeutic effect on me, because I could identify the feelings I had and was able to examine and then deal with them. They were often fleeting emotions and the poetry was a form of medicine.
Sometimes the poems came to me as I carried out a mundane task, such as ironing or changing bed linen.

I cried into my ironing today was one such poem. The sudden and unexpected surge of sadness I felt here was so strong that the only way I could understand what was happening was to write those feelings down.

Other people will have had other ways of coping during this period, I am sure. And many people had to carry on with an attempt at normality, if they were on the front line in essential occupations such as nursing. Like many others, I am still thankful to these people. It was like a war situation, but we were fighting an unseen enemy.

Memories of Svalbard

I think back to all those years ago
When our solitary ship
Ploughed through icy waters
Bound for Svalbard and the receding ice.

Ice floes were there of course
But in smaller numbers
And only a shadow of their former selves
Clinging on in desperation.
We gasped in admiration
And soaked in the turquoise seas
The magnificent scenery that we'd paid to see.
We washed our hands at the door
To ward off the threat of a floating sanitarium.

In the stately room we gathered.
Focused intently on the words
Of the expert glaciologist
The man with the answers.

He spoke with enthusiasm
Infecting us with the knowledge
He'd accumulated over years.
And then the devastating words
That come back to haunt us now.
'Don't worry. Climate change won't get us.
The next pandemic will.'

Frozen in Time

My days are different now.
I do not drift unthinkingly
From one hour to the next.
Instead I measure my life.
I break it up into Bitesize chunks.

Each bit has far more value
Even as I do mundane tasks
Like change the bed
Or steam clean the floor
To ward off the silent enemy.

I wonder whether I can be sure
The sewing task I set myself
Will ever be finished.
I hope it will.
The morass of photographs I lift
From the box beneath the bed
Take on a wider significance now.
And I study each one intently
Trying to recall the exact time
The shutter clicked.
That precious moment frozen in time.

A meeting with friends at 5 o'clock prompt
Takes on the importance of a virtual G20 summit.
We laugh, we share.
And the next one is scheduled with uncertain certainty.
Kaleidoscopic patterns
That are shaken by the day's events.
This is the unbidden world
Of the latest pandemic.

I cried into my ironing today

I cried tears into my ironing today.
They fell silently, relentlessly.
The stubbornness of them surprised me.
They refused to stop.
Continued unabated.
Even when I left to walk upstairs
They followed me.
And my mood was one of sombre resignation.
I wallowed in the pits of helpless,
Hopeless tears.

I think it was the never-endingness,
The not-knowingness.
The life that stretches out ahead
With seemingly no change in view.

The tentacles wrapped round me
Gripping me with fierce intent.
Refusing to let me free.
Like the virus itself.

I slept a thousand days today,
I dreamt a thousand dreams.
And relieved I woke to yet another day.
They will return those tears.
And when they do I'll be prepared.
More resilient.
More resolute.
More ready.

That's only what I hope.
And hope can change so easily to tears.

This different world

The days swim together now
No longer separated by meaningful dates
On a calendar made obsolete and sad.
I adjust a painting on the wall
As if it were a matter of life and death.
We are living through history.

I stare mournfully through a window
And fixate on two small shapes
On the far side of an empty field.
Mountain hares venturing closer
Than they ever would have dared
Unless shielded by the protective
Shadows of the night.

A heron lands gently, surveying. Still.
In a space it would never
Before have landed.
Confident it cannot be disturbed
In this place where time stands still.

And I dare to think of future times.
And know for certainty
That a new normal is taking shape.
I reach that calm acceptance.
And in this moment, for me at least
A new beginning stirs.
The past has faded
And we live in a strange
And different world.

This time last year

This time last year the boats set sail.
They cruised the seas
In thoughtless exploration of foreign lands.
This time last year the air space filled
From north to south, from east to west
Stretching across the globe
With no restrictions.
Nothing out of bounds.

This time this year the world itself has shrunk.
We look inwards not outwards
The harbours silent, the airports dead.
The sights and sounds of foreign lands
Come only through bright screens,
Experiences vicariously numbed in isolation.

This time next year
Well who can say?
We dare not guess. Choose not to.
In case by guessing
We predict a future
None of us would choose to see.

Riverside Walk

Riverside walkers wear a mask of fear
As they pass each other cautiously
on their single designated walk.
Sometimes a rare smile breaks through
And words of false cheerfulness slice through the air.
An attempt at normality.
An atmosphere of foreboding, not knowing;
a blanket of resigned acceptance of the way things are,
of the way things have to be.

On the river, a rare merganser
takes advantage of the silent day.
Lifting off and skimming skilfully over the silver water.
Snowdrops group in comforting clusters.
And late daffodils begin to nod.
Not with the joyfulness of Wordsworth's blooms.
But with another message.
A desperate plea that the world's natural cycle
Will not be broken
By the Dance of Death.

The name I dare not speak

I hardly dare speak the name
Coronavirus 19.
It's taken over my working day
And sometimes deep into the night.
It consumes my restless mind
Like an alien creature
From a science fiction world.

It eats into the inner parts
Stubbornly refusing to give any space
To brighter thoughts
That once took hold.
The coup was quick,
Impossible to stop
There was no warning.

One day my mind was free.
I went about my life in blissful unawareness.
With normal hopes and fears of course
But everything a challenge,
Nothing insurmountable.
A rollercoaster life that stretched ahead.

I'm powerless now I sense
I can't predict a future
But cling to science fiction cures.
The elixir of a vaccine not too far away.
Coronavirus 19.
I speak the name out loud.

Our Sterile Room

We live a sterile life,
A life devoid of colour.
The palette laid out before us.
Our walls reflecting nothing back.
We are forced to reassess.

And with that reassessment
Comes the gradual realisation
That things can change.
We are the clichéd masters of our destiny.
We turn the wheel to steer a different course.

We start to see where colours are.
The tiny things we missed before.
A conversation hanging in the air
With a passing stranger.
The flight of a pheasant
Disturbed from the undergrowth.
A hairy insect crawling laboriously
Across a gravel path.

We find our oxygen
Not in the lifeless screen
That dominates a corner of the sterile room
But in the sounds and sights
We missed before.
We gulp the air and breathe.

Operation Vaccination

Like a military operation,
Each car directed to a safe spot
By men in orange jackets.
An army of volunteers who'd been trained
To ease the flow of traffic.
To reassure the nervous,
Inspire with confidence,
Direct the unsure.
From a place of uncertainty and hesitation
To a more hopeful future.

I followed the arrows
That led me to the echo of a school gym
Now emptied of the youthful shouts and squeals.
The buzz of activity
Replaced by an older generation,
Eager to receive the first dose
Of a vaccine that would transform their lives.
Erase the horror.

We lined up dutifully
Stepped forward on instruction.
And with nervous conversations
Accepted what was offered.
The mood changed.
We visibly relaxed,
Exchanging one life for the promise of another.

Night Sky

I'm gazing at the night sky tonight
Hoping to find solace in the stars.
An ebony blanket far above me
Peppered with shining points of light.
I search for the promised movement
Of forty meteorites tracing a path
At roughly thirty second intervals.
An earthly intrusion that seems out of place
For this moment at least.

There is no comfort in the stars for me
Though there might have been at other times.
I only see a distant world
That I am not a part of.
A world that screams my mortality
And writes it large across the sky
Like an advertiser's banner.
You are not one of us.
You are mortal and frail and weak.

Then just as I am about to turn away
I see the flash of a distant meteor.
Cosmic dust burning its shining path
And disappearing without a trace.
And I know that meteor's me.
I turn and look away.
That second is all I need for now.

Seize the Day

I long for those days,
Of long walks, of jokes and laughter by the sea.
Our lives entwined and shared.
The ease with which we trod the paths of friendship.
The sleepy awakening
To days that were filled with fun.
Seven days in November
In a house that echoed with footsteps
Of generations of friends and families past.

Those paths we trod unthinkingly
Darting from one conversation to the next
Unaware that things would change
That hollow laughs would only come
From an echo on a screen.
An artificial meeting scheduled
To try to keep the links.
The fragile chain that must not break.

They might return, those days,
And when they do
We'll understand them more.
We'll oil the chain of friendship
With more clarity
And more awareness
Of how easily those links can break.
We'll seize the days.

Forest Walk

I saw someone touch a leaf today
In the birch wood by the river.
They held it gently in their hand
As I held my breath and watched.
A silent observer of a private scene
Trespassing on that moment
Meant for no one but herself to see.

I'm not sure what it might signify
That moment by the river.
Perhaps the stranger's thoughts were similar
To those that crossed my mind.
That the leaf could bring some comfort
To the times that we now knew.
Or perhaps thoughts strayed to loved ones
Far away and far from touch.
That the life we were observing
Was the preciousness we found
In the birch tree by the river
And the silence all around.

I turned and faced the other way
Connecting with the light.
And I trod the path in silence
As the river filled my mind.

People

The poems here contain personal pen portraits of people who have made strong impressions on me, both as a child or in my adult life. Some of them helped to shape the person I became and I remember them all with love and gratitude.

My Blackpool Grandma was the first of these influences, as most of my childhood summer holidays were spent in her company. I was regarded as a delicate child, prone to illness, so I was duly bundled off every July to the seaside town of Blackpool to recuperate and become stronger; I returned fit enough to face the coming harsh winters of an industrial Manchester.

My Grandma took her role in this very seriously. I became her project. She nurtured me with firm but loving care, teaching me many of her traditional skills along the way. The weekdays were organised regimentally and we never deviated. Evenings were spent in quiet companionship. These weeks also gave me the chance to hear many stories of her life, which sounded so much more interesting than mine.

Another major influence was my older brother Peter, to whom I attached myself from an early age. I trailed after him constantly and he accepted my presence with patience and generous good humour. He was almost 5 years older than me and only now can I begin to imagine how he must have felt, as an older teenager watching over a younger sibling. I feel so fortunate to have had him in my life and I hope the poems reflect that.

You will notice that other poems in this section are about situations or people that just appeared in my life momentarily. I tried to capture some everyday encounters that struck me as worth recording, either because they highlighted interesting behaviour or because I wanted to prolong the memory.

The poem *Skipping Rope Blues* brings to life the street games that I now see less and less, as children become more dependent on technology for entertainment. Again, this was something that was affected by the pandemic. There is definitely an aura of nostalgia here.

Finally, this is an attempt to keep my memories alive. I hope readers will enjoy the reflective nature of this part of the anthology. Perhaps it will prompt you to look back on your own life and recognise similar situations.

My Buxom Blackpool Grandma

We shared a bond
My buxom Blackpool Grandma and me
As every summer I left the city streets
To spend my weeks in the seaside air
Of the town where I'd been born.
A frail, pale child.
Gaining strength to combat the damp fog
Of a Manchester winter.

On Mondays we folded sheets meticulously,
Taking a corner each
And ironing the creases out of the cotton and my life.
We shelled the peas together
At a wooden table, scrubbed and clean
In a kitchen devoid of gadgets.

My stern-faced Grandma taught me how to knit
And I helped to make rag rugs
That proudly adorned her flat.
Twice a week we caught the tram
That shunted us to the picture house
Where we shared a passion.
I wallowed in the Shane of Alan Ladd
And was mesmerised by Audrey Hepburn
In the Moon River film
That was Breakfast at Tiffany's.

In the evenings the cards were taken out
Or dominoes were shaken from the biscuit tin
That lay hidden in the drawer of the old dresser..
And at 9.30 precisely we laid the table
For our ritual supper.
Cream crackers (only Jacob's of course)
Washed down with a pot of glorious tea.
Just me and Mary Jane
The Blackpool Grandma I adored.

Skipping Rope Blues

Those memories aren't fading now
But become clearer as the mists of time
Lift and disappear, revealing moving tableaux.
The first shows Kathleen Taylor
Gripping one end of the snake rope,
Which stretched across the road
Tied to a lamppost in the fading light.
A rhythmic motion, whirring sounds
Of 'I am a girl-guide dressed in blue.
These are the things that I can do.'
And me leaping over the rope.
Nimble, assured, balletic.
The playground was the street
That we spilled onto,
United in our vision of freedom and adventure
A towering cotton mill watched over us
And childish screams of laughter
Echoed across the valley.

Those days felt endless then
When the grating sound of roller skates
Took over from the skipping rope
As we twirled or danced on one leg,
Each of us determined
To be the star of the show,
To receive the accolades
Before we were called in, protesting at the appointed hour.

The second was the day I was crowned May Queen.
A coveted prize, long awaited
That only came round once.
I sat regally on a throne
On a decorated open wagon.
Drenched by torrential rain,
Surrounded by unhappy handmaidens.
I watched as my paper flowers
Got soggier and soggier and I wept
Tears of disappointment, when my spring smiles
Disappeared with the tissue paper roses.

The third was the memory of opening the letter
The one that directed us to two fates.
And seeing the widespread smiles
The clap on the back, the relief
Of passing the exam that opened up the world.
Or so it seemed to us at eleven.

And at the other end of the street
Stood Kathleen Taylor.
Disappointed, forlorn, separate.
We dropped the ends of the rope
And sadly walked in opposite directions.

My Brother's Birthday

My brother's eighty next week
And I can't quite believe it.
I've known him for over seventy-five years.
That doesn't seem possible.
But of course it is.
The birth certificates prove it.

In the fifties we watched tv
On a grainy tv screen too small to see
Black and white images firing the imagination
And a coronation gripping the nation.
Not on a Sunday though
When the pottery wheel mesmerised.
When we climbed instead to Hartshead Pike
To kick a ball outside The Hare and Hounds
Bribed with a packet of crisps and a bottle of pop.
Nothing sophisticated for us Mossley kids.

At other times, my brother took me
To strange places like the Unitarian Church
To join a youth club.
But only so we could play table tennis or snooker.
Not for spiritual salvation.
Not for the sixties generation.

Sometimes we went to Old Trafford
To watch George Best do his magic.
And once I went to a jazz club.
A younger sister dragged along
Because he had no choice.
A smokey dive of a place in Oldham.
And though I'd begged him to take me
I really only craved The Beatles.

Not everything went smoothly though.
Like the time they left us in charge
And we thought it a good idea to read the papers
While a chip pan crackled unnoticed
And a kitchen erupted into flames.
Nobody hurt though. So all was forgiven.
And anyway the insurance paid.

Down all those years I don't remember
A cross word being spoken
Not between us anyway.
Though that could be false memory.

I loved my brother and I still do.
We shared some special times.
And I thank him for that with all my heart.
So Happy Birthday Brother.
Rock on.

Pam xx

Peter, my big brother

My lovely brother lost his brave fight today
And a piece of me broke off.
I'll never see that face again
Or hear the voice or watch the smile.
But the memories will remain
And I'll make sure that those don't fade.

No one can erase the person he became.
A larger than life family man
A character with a personality to match.
And a wise, sardonic view of the world
Built on a wealth of encounters.
Experiences too many to mention.

In later years we didn't meet
As often as we'd have liked.
The Irish Sea a barrier to sibling love
But the strong bond remained
That closeness never shattered.

And I hope he knew how much that meant
The shared childhood, the friends we became.
Because to me that's precious
And helps me bear the heartbreak
That I now feel.

Mick

Life hangs on the finest thread
Like the delicate silver wisp
Of a spider's web
Dangling precariously from darkened skies.
One minute a recuperating stroll
Round a favourite lakeside haunt,
The next a faded video
A melodic soulful voice
Reaching out to friends with Ebony Eyes
Across an untouchable divide.

Memories bind and connect
A friend universally treasured
Remembered for the verbal colour he brought
To our black and white world.
The laughs that echoed
Spreading a smile from face to dampened face.

Even as we say goodbye
The smiles remain
Shared memories that span the years.
And laughter tinkles musically
Across that crowded room
Connecting the unconnected.

Thank you Mick for all you gave.
We will remember.
And be forever grateful
That our paths crossed.

Fab Four

We met just 60 years ago this week,
And bathed luxuriously
In the newfound freedoms
Of lives lived far away from home.
Freed to explore new ground,
Forge friendships based on shared interests
And views of a world that resonated
With us, the 'sixties kids.
We found fresh paths to tread
In a wide-eyed world of loves won and lost.
Set against a background of Beatles, Beach Boys
And Rolling Stones.
None of us realising then
That we were our own travelling troubadours.

We danced together at the freshers' disco
Moving to the rhythmic beats of Status Quo
Who belted out their Matchstick Men
To a captive throng.
Our first chance to laugh and share
Lighthearted observations of newfound liberty.
Slowly, tentatively
Inching our way into an adult world.

Whoever knew then that sixty years on
Our own Fab Four would meet again
To wind our way through woodland paths
In September sunshine?
Sharing sixty years of mixed memories.
Still wanting to look back and laugh
At dreams we had and made come true.
Of stumbles along the way.
Searching for more awesome adventure.
Appreciating the past
But not encased by it.
Warmed by the cloaks of friendship.
Lives still lived and loved.

A cold wet Thursday in Grantown

Surrounded by a group of Americans today
As we sat in comfort in the High Street Cafe,
Our usual haunt on a cold wet Thursday.
All asking for takeouts they filled the space.
The usual calm disturbed by clashing voices.

Alien accents cut through the air
And prejudices surfaced in the blink of an eye.
Off to Aberdeen and Balmoral
To glimpse a royal at fifty paces.
The usual tourist trap.

'What a quiet village this is!' one yelled,
Unaware of any irony in the words.
An attempt to engage two friends
Seated like us in a favourite window spot,
Hoping perhaps for privacy and calm
But replying patiently with
'Aye - a Victorian town, hen; it's nae a village.'

At last the wind blew in and they blew out.
Loaded down with cream cakes and coffee
And heading for the Granite City
And the magnet of the tourist trail.
Leaving us all to our wry smiles
And a second cappuccino.

Caryl

It's so hard to describe
A friend like Caryl.
Someone I've only known
For a short time
But seem to have known forever.

Slipping into friendship was easy
Like sliding into calm waters.
No effort needed.
No resistance felt.
'A friend behind a stranger's face'
As Maya Angelou once said.

A few tentative exchanges
Over favourite books
And then suddenly nothing is off the table.
A mind alert and ready
To explore a complex world.
From a life enriched by personal stories.
Distant lands visited.
Experiences painted from a palette
That any artist would envy.

And a listener too.
Not too common in this Trump world.
Someone who listens with the heart.
Radiating warmth with every breath.
Shared laughter drifting on the breeze.

My Grandma's Story

The needles clicked rhythmically
A sharp metallic sound
Breaking the silence of a Sunday night.
And my thoughts returned to other Sundays
Years ago and almost forgotten.
When I held the hanks of wool
Positioned between outstretched arms
As my Grandma patiently, meticulously
Rewound the wool to form balls
That could then be used
To make the jumper that I'd begged her for.

And as we worked in unison
She'd spin the tales of her own youth
When she worked in service
For someone else
More privileged, more comfortable.
Someone who could afford to employ
A young girl from Bishop Auckland
And generously allow her to go home
One precious day for Mothering Sunday.

She spoke and I created a garment
Made up of scraps of her life
A world away from mine.
A patchwork of events.
Images of people I'd never met
Of places I'd never known.

I looked down at my own work now
And as the needles clicked
I wondered who would piece together
The fabric of my life.
My story.

Pat

How do I begin to describe Pat?
Where do I start?
I first met Pat at Wingfield School
A small Comprehensive on the edge of Rotherham.
She was my first Head of Department
And I was a young PE teacher fresh from College.
I could not have been more lucky.

Pat taught me things I never learned
From hours of lectures in the History
Or Philosophy or Psychology of Education.
Things you can't learn from books.
She led by example and I tentatively
Tried to follow in her footsteps.
She approached everything with humour,
A ready smile diffusing any tense standoff.
And above all the children knew
That Pat (like Mrs Kaye in Our Day Out)
Was definitely on their side.

I remember cold Saturday mornings
Of hockey, netball or rounders matches
To places like Kimberworth, Maltby or Wath-on-Dearne
Athletic meets that cut long into the day
Coaches with steaming windows and excited voices.
All organised like clockwork and run without question.
Pat always encouraging and cheering from the sidelines
Commiserating when needed.
A reputation for fairness
A respect that spread through city schools.

But more than that
And most important of all to me
Was the friendship that endured
Down all the years
A sunny optimism, a helping hand,
A ready listener.
I feel privileged to have known Pat Robson
And to count her my friend.
To have shared some of her stories
Of family life with Mick and Nathan, Anne and Maya.
Of travels to France and far more besides.

I will remember Pat as a shining star
That lit the room she entered - a Super Nova.
Making the world we inhabit seem a better place.
Thank you Pat.

Snowflakes

A Wednesday morning in November.
Listening to the soft tones
That signal the start of Tai Chi.
Words that envelop me gently
And accompany the rhythmic moves
Of The Form in all its complex simplicity.

Snow is falling beyond the windows,
A perfect backdrop to the scene.
Anxiety melts away with the moves.
Gentle encouragement the only sound
That breaks the Golden Silence.
Feathers of light float around;
Perfect symmetry in the turns.

The world and its woes recede
And in peaceful unison we face
An unknown enemy.
Singly and together we focus on a space,
Pushing and yielding with quiet dignity.
A musical accompaniment to the falling snow.
Alone and together
In a field of dreams.

CD Necklace

A collection of old CDs
Danced on string across the garden gate,
Catching the afternoon sun
In the clear autumnal sky.
A myriad of rainbow colours
Glinting before my eyes
And I caught the writing
As they twisted and turned in the gentle breeze.

A felt-tipped message of '60s and '70s
Favourite collections from a distant time
Like an old necklace too dated to wear.
And across the leaf-strewn lawn
I watched the arrow of a dragonfly
Haphazardly searching for somewhere to land
Blue wings whirring softly.
And the brown leaves on the grass
Waiting to be whipped up and shifted
To heaps beneath the dying beech hedge.

I tried to recall the tracks I'd recorded
The anthems of youth now faded memories.
But instead only focused on the dried leaves
That seemed to reflect my inner thoughts.
Lacking in life and of no use.
For now the CDs will just need to dance
In an empty space.

Thoughts on Age

Why is it that, as the years pass by,
I start to notice the smaller things?
Not just life's bends and turns
And twists that catch us woefully unawares.
But the smaller things
That have been there beside us all along.

A bright yellow forsythia
Reaching up hopefully to the azure sky;
A rich brown bumblebee cruising purposefully
Between delicate Snake's Head Fritillary
In search of sustenance.
Or the majestic buzzard high overhead,
Circling above me
On its own desperate search for moving prey below.
Keen eyes passed down through generations
Of raptors that came before.

And I dwell on my own history.
Disappearing links in a chain
Of unrecognisable past.
People who dreamed of a better world
For their own offspring,
Not knowing what future
They would need to face.
In a world where trees and bees and all things natural
Would fade into the mists of time.
As they themselves have done.

Old photographs staring out unknowingly
In awe of a space age new technology.
That captures our minds in its iron grip
And forces out the natural world.
In all its glorious variety.

And which I now know for sure
Is why I'm compelled to notice these smaller things.
Before they fade forever.
Smaller, yes.
But beautiful and calming.
And vital.

Letter to Rachel Carson

You warned us all in 1962
And stubbornly we refused to listen.
When the signs were all around,
The evidence was clear.

Cheerfully we continued on our way,
Marketing the pesticides
That would lead inexorably
To a Silent Spring
And all in the name of Progress.

The Silent Spring is closer now,
Creeping relentlessly to a deathly end
Where no birds sing
And we move around this earth
In desperate isolation.

Time is running short now Rachel
And maybe our children see
What we refused to see.
They give you voice
And look to a future
Where dollars matter less
Than that precious blue dot
Suspended in the arc of time.

We, the Watchers

Here I have selected poems that focus on the natural world and its interdependence. Biodiversity is such a crucial part of our existence and these poems attempt to home in on that.

There are poems about insects, birds, trees and mammals, many of them inspired by a single moment, as I observed from a distance – poems such as *Sky Dance, Fox Family and Eagle Eyes.* Sometimes the moments captured were scenes viewed from a bedroom window during a sleepless night or just events experienced walking or cycling along local paths, alone or with others.

Also included here are some poems which highlight habitat loss, such as *The Hoolock Gibbon - a story of our time.* I wrote this after reading about a situation taking place in a remote village in northeast India, where the number of a troop of rare gibbons was down to only 20, with 4 breeding females. Villagers were so desperate to save these creatures that they shared their meagre food supplies with them and monitored them daily. They recognised the richness of sharing their world with this endangered species. This is something we may only realise ourselves when such species no longer exist.

There is a recurrent theme running through these poems: it is an attempt to capture and celebrate the variety of life that we still have on the Goldilocks planet we call home. I hope you will recognise some of the special moments recorded in the anthology, add your voice to those trying to protect the natural world and take pleasure in reading them.

Sky Dance

An aerial display
An ever-changing shape
Morphing as they swept and swerved
Across the mid-day canvas
Of a clear blue winter sky.

We watched, entranced,
Absorbed in the ritual.
Unable to understand the how or why.
But in awe of this collective dance.

These lapwings are oblivious
To the four of us below
We do not signify
In their mesmeric world.
And neither should we.

They are the masters.
We do not count in their feathered world.
Our insignificance
Is palpable.

But in that moment
We, the watchers, were as one.
United by chance alone.
We laughed our delight.
Strangers who looked upwards
And for one eternal moment
Shared in that dance
And lived.

Eagle Eyes

Eagle eyes scour the land below
Soaring on wings of powerful beauty.
Searching for mountain hares
In an ever diminishing world.
A world we've helped to shape
Mass trespassed to the point of destruction.

We in our own sphere search the skies
And shuffle along our personal paths.
A graceful swallow dips and dives
The mournful cuckoo echoes across the valley.
And we find no answers.

First tentative steps as we exit lockdown
A desperate attempt to find new norms.
An exploration of an interlocking globe.
Our environment malfunctioning.
Short-term solutions to long-term problems.

Politicians feeding us on useless sound bites
Naive ignorance of the power of Nature.
We grope in the dark
We stumble and fall.
We head blindly to our unknown destination.

View From Space

I look up at the cloudless sky
And see the moon suspended
Like a stray bauble left over
From the Christmas celebrations.
And I wonder how Tim Peake must feel
Now that he's back on Planet Earth.
I sense his disappointment
As he looks around him, knowing
That we do not value as he values
The scene around us,
The creatures that surround us.

We do not see the pale blue dot
As he once did. Delicate. Fragile.
Nor do we appreciate the uniqueness
Of this place. The frailty of home.
We haven't had his vantage point.
The lens we use is a closeup lens.
Our only focus is the here and now.
And not the distant future.

I point my camera at the woodland pond
Where reflections of trees are mirrored.
I know this image will disappear with time.
And so will the aching beauty
That we once called Earth.

Dark Green Fritillary

Two toned sprite dancing across the Moor
Wisp of a butterfly, light as a feather
Purple heather, fans of orange wings.
Purposeful, beautiful, oblivious of us.

Focus on this.
Watch the patterns of flight, as they skip and skate
Across Tulloch Moor.
Feathered hairy tube of a body
Probing needles balancing gently
Disturbing nothing, single-minded.
Focused.

We watch entranced.
From our ringside seat,
The boulder nestling in the heather.
No sound breaks the heavenly silence.

Dark green fritillary.
Nymphalidea: Speyaria aglaia.
In that moment nothing else matters.
We drink the nectar.
As Time stands still.

Willow Warbler

The shrub was overgrown and scraggy,
Golden flowers cringing sadly behind it.
Shears were out, ruthlessly pruning.

Some birds set up the warning screech
Hopping frantically from branch to branch.
Impotent, helpless, watching.

And then all was revealed.
The hidden refuge that had been the nest.
And concealed therein the treasure trove.
The unhatched eggs of another generation.

Shears hastily abandoned. Branches pieced together.
The home rebuilt.
At last the noise subsided.
A guilty retreat.
I hope the nest was saved.
I hope I sleep tonight.

Night Visitor

Jupiter and Saturn were aligned tonight
Forming a strange shape in the night sky.
The wind rocked me awake
So I opened the window
To stare and focus on the street below.
A different stage set from the daytime world.

And out of the blackness
A second shape emerged
Compact and round and in motion.
Gliding quickly and purposefully
From light to dark
As it moved across the stage.

For one moment unrecognisable
Till childhood memories surfaced.
A shape familiar to all children
But now just rarely seen.
The hedgehog of Beatrix Potter fame.
A sign of hope in today's darkness.
A fleeting glimpse of what should be.
Silently I closed the window
And left my prickly friend
To her nocturnal world.

Fox Family

I saw you once
A family of four that viewed the garden as its own.
Deep into the night.
Moon illuminating carefree play.
I wanted to join you, share you, cherish you.
But instead I watched in hushed silence
In awe from an upstairs window.

Nothing should destroy the serenity
Of that intimate family scene
No one has the right.
The earth was yours.
The earth should be yours.
We need only watch from afar
On a moonlit night in November.

Thoughts on Sheffield

I trudge familiar streets
But I'm in an unfamiliar landscape
A hostile place
Where heads are down
Searching silver screens.
Where no one smiles
Or connects anymore.
Engrossed in the trivia of a digital world.
Horns blare as traffic builds
And tempers rise in the manic rush
To get from place to place.
Yes, autumn leaves surround us
But who bothers to look up?

A kingfisher flashes metallic blue
Skimming the murky water
Ignored by walking robots
Who prefer to share a TikTok video.
A depressing place of throwaway drinks
Deliveroo and Just Eat the new Utopia.
Cardboard boxes discarded freely
Kicked along with golden leaves.

I turn away and choose a different path
Where skies are big and mountains soar
A place where eagles draw the eye
Where eyes look up not down.

35   The Hoolock Gibbon
– a story of our times

Has anyone even heard of the Hoolock Gibbon?
I doubt it very much.
They're not the first species
That come to mind
When you're thinking of the Red List, are they?
But they're wild and wonderful and awesome creatures.

The Hoolock Gibbon lives in a remote place
A tiny enclave in North East India.
That goes by the name of Barakuri.
Currently consisting of only twenty gibbons in number.
With just four adult females to give them frail hope.
It's a race against time.
And it's a race they're not going to win.
Villagers watch as the Gibbons swing happily through the sparse forest.
Skilful and agile, watchful and caring.
Assisted by a handful of humans
Who are thankful to share their space
With a different species.
People who eagerly supplement a meagre diet
By offering the Gibbons bananas or other fruits.
Farmers like fifty-five-year-old
Mohit Chuchia,
An unsung hero,
Who tends to the Gibbons as well as his own family.
And the Gibbons respond
By singing their thanks with a haunting chorus
That travels like magic through the forest.

But desperate times draw near for the Hoolock Gibbon.
Trees spell wealth and oil drills ravage the land.
Electricity cables cause injury, death and destruction.
And as always
Profit, power and poverty rule.

So it isn't a story
That we know will end well.
We can only watch and wait and admire
This small group of amazing social creatures.
And praise those people who do everything
To make sure that we at least know about
The wonderful existence
Of the Hoolock Gibbons.
Before they disappear from this earth.
Remember their name well.
Because that's all we'll have.

The Kite

I watched a kite flying high today,
Tugging at the string so tightly grasped
By inexperienced but hopeful hands.
Soaring to reach a freer place
But instantly denied.

Delighted squeals and whoops of joy
Drifted in the clear air
And proud faces watched and urged him on.

Sometimes in our life we mimic the kite
As we strive for that better place.
Hoping for a way
That releases us from the grind
That pins us daily to the ground.

And when we do reach those places
They should be shared and valued
By those who might have held the string
Or tried to steer us to the paths
That they preferred to follow.

That kite did reach a higher place
The string extended to its furthest point
As it streamed across the sky
Trailing coloured ribbons in its wake.

And the hands that held it
Followed wherever it led
Face uplifted in awe and wonder.
That moment will stay with him forever
And I'm pleased to say
I shared it too.

37 Nethy to Grantown Bike Ride

A feeling of freedom
Hardly a breath of wind.
Feet pushing hard against pedals of steel.
Always present.
And the first sighting of lapwing
Fluttering and skittish in distant fields.
Time-honoured honking of greylag geese
And the nervous flight of golden-eye
Never trusting. Ever watchful.
Transient in the river
As they search for a spot
Less disturbed by humankind.

And on the way back a lucky sight
In the rolling meadow by the farmyard track.
A hare, bounding and leaping.
Fear, the fuel for that restless energy.
Its white tail signalling its whereabouts
As it glides with relief
Into the field beyond our view.
A privilege to observe.
The curtain call of Nature.

The Mountain Ash

It's almost November in the Cairngorms
And against all the odds
I'm looking at the rich red berries
Of the Rowan tree,
Clinging tenaciously
To the outline of their stark,
Bare, branches.

Somehow the tree symbolises
The way we feel.
Desperate to cling onto
Those thin watery rays of summer
Before we're swept roughly
Into the grey dark days
Of a Highland winter.

No evidence yet of fieldfare or redwing
Swarming in to feed on the richness
Of autumn's bounty.
Yet still tempting, expectant, hopeful.
As the ruby jewels take centre stage.

And we sense that one strong wind
Will fiercely denude
Those skeleton branches.
So I watch and bathe in the beauty
Of those berries
For just one more glorious day.

Nature's Balm

I sank gratefully onto a garden bench
That gave unrestricted views
Of the meadow and mountains beyond.
And I was empowered.

The calm of the natural world
Was the balm the spirit needed
And a gentle, pastoral scene
Unfolded before my eyes.

Lambs snuggled contentedly against protective, wary ewes.
An orchestra of birdsong surrounded and caressed me
And I breathed in the freshness of a damp May morning.

In the distance a male pheasant stalked the tall grasses.
The misty blue mountains formed a beckoning backdrop.
I breathed in deeply as the breeze caressed my face
And anxiety melted away.

A Close Encounter

We edged further into the deep forest
Wheels turning slowly as we gained height.
Eyes warily scanning the winding path ahead
And the dark protection of the canopy above.

Hearts racing.
Few noises around us.
Just the soft crackle of needle carpet
And a gentle wind whistling
As we pressed on further.
Then suddenly he was there.
A dark, huddled shape, nestled in the crook of two branches.
Waiting, watchful, ready.
A few seconds passed, seeming like hours
Then with a wild clattering of wings
A determined swoop arcing perfectly
To land square and solid
Facing us on the path ahead.
Blocking the route,
A menacing combatant
Iconic tail feathers spread like a magnificent fan.
Ready for action.
We were trespassers. This was his patch.
His territory.
He faced an enemy of intruders.
And they were not welcome.

Splashes of red and white adorned the plumage.
More useful armour to add to the needle beak
And curved talons, that could be brought into action
To startle and surprise.

We lingered no more as he advanced slowly towards us,
We turned the wheels in unison
To beat a hasty retreat.
The Capercaillie had won his most recent battle.
And we left him to his domain.
With memories forever of our beautiful encounter
With the legendary Horse of the Woods.
Driven to near extinction by the hands of men.

The Meadow

The meadow was mown for money today.
Clover, cowslips and caterpillars
Cut to make way for caravans
And a campervan invasion
For one dark week in June.
This precious habitat destroyed
In a single hour.

We can't replace that home
And the life dependent on it.
They have no voices to object.
We are their collective voice
And we choose to remain mute
In the face of all the mayhem.

But profit trumps all, it seems
And perhaps the world will realise
When all these creatures disappear
Only to be found in faded picture books
And old photos in forgotten albums.

I can only watch
The rhythmic tractor in the meadow
As the life beneath it dies.
And as the sun sets
My own heart sinks with it.

The Treasures of the Mind

The warmth bathes my skin
As I point my face
With closed eyes
In the direction of the low winter sun.

Nothing stirs
But the gentle flap of a pigeon's wings
And the harsh familiar croak
Of the watchful crow
Sitting in the pines
Behind my garden bench.

If I strain I can hear
The distant drone of traffic
Or Dave's dogs on their daily round.
But I shut these out
And concentrate alone
On the still soft sounds
That surround me now
And transport me to a faraway place
Where water laps white sand
Or green valleys stretch for miles
Into unexplored wilderness.

They're the treasures of the mind,
So I preciously clutch them.
And tell no one.

Winners and Losers

In the murky darkness of the garden pond
I spotted the black shapes
Recognisable as tadpoles.
No longer full stops in a sea of jelly
But transformed as they darted and dashed.
One moment tight against the rock,
The next in the open, nibbling frantically
At the floating leaves or stalks
That would sustain their fragile lives.
Aiding their transition into adult frogs
That would explore and roam.
A success story in the making.

Further up the garden, hiding shyly
An injured wood pigeon, dragging a wing
As it limped along in a desperate effort
To survive with damaged limb.
Slim chance but with a natural instinct
To beat the odds and recover
Before a predatory cat or sparrow hawk
In its own search for food
Cuts short its life.
Winners and losers.
Not all of us get to choose.

On Geese Flying

I watched a skein of geese today
As they flew high above the window
In their silent V formation
Being pulled by an invisible magnet
Towards a summer homeland
In Iceland, Greenland
Or the shores of Svalbard.

They changed formation easily
As bird after bird took the lead
One dropping back to give space
To the next one who had the strength
To meet the forces of nature head-on.

I never cease to wonder
At their silent communication
Passed on from generation to generation.
They know where they came from
And they're sure of where they're going.

Unlike us, the human race
Whose story is told in a fabric of lies
Woven by those whose interests are served
By concealing the truth.

And there's no way of knowing
Just where we're heading
So we'll watch the last geese fly.

Acknowledgements

Many thanks to my friend, Gill Warren, who has waved her magic wand from the other side of the world to turn the dream of this anthology into an actual book.

To my editor and publisher, Mick Le Moignan, of Bouley Bay Books, whose advice has been invaluable, and to Trish Le Moignan, for the beautiful cover.

And last but by no means least, to my wonderful husband, Steve, for sharing the paths less trodden and for your love and encouragement over 60 years.

About the Author – Pam Ward

Pam was born in Blackpool in 1946 but spent her childhood in Mossley, near Manchester. In 1965, she moved across the Pennines to Sheffield, where she qualified as a teacher of English and PE. Here, she and her husband Steve settled and brought up their family of two daughters, while continuing to teach in inner-city schools. As a mature student, Pam gained an MA in Communication from Sheffield Hallam University.

For many years she worked as an external examiner for GCSE English Literature, writing poetry in her leisure time. On retirement, Pam and Steve moved to a remote village in the Scottish Highlands. Here, she and her husband cycle the mountain and forest trails of the Cairngorm National Park and she continues to write poetry, which has been her passion since childhood. Her poems are often inspired by the natural world.

www.ingramcontent.com/pod-product-compliance
Lightning Source LLC
Chambersburg PA
CBHW062054290426
44109CB00027B/2821